THE RISING

Finding My Voice

Sergiy Abelson

A collection of poetry written by Sergiy Abelson.
Original artwork by Sergiy Abelson.

May you find your voice.

Rise above the crowds.

Yell at the top of your lungs.

And teach your heart to beat harder

and faster

For love.

Content warning

Suicidal ideation
Self harm
Sexual trauma
Violence
Eating disorders
Substance Use Disorder
Religious abuse and trauma

To Mr. Al Squires, Sarah Knowles Barrett, and all of MedEx Tier IV Summer 2022

Alycia Perez-Johnson	*Tori Kellog*
Caroline Loftus	*Jenna Seubarran*
Haley Hirth	*Blake Martin*
Ambrasia Fuller	*Amanda McGowan*
Antonia Gacha	*Aryn Akerberg*
Bryan Lopez-Montoya	*Courtney Weber*
Elizabeth Panarrieta-Flores	*Gabrielle Fedel*
Guillana Socorro	*Isabelle McDaniel*
Isabelle McDaniel	*Jennifer Kidane*
Jordan Rucker	*Joshua Manuel-Venegas*
Judah Smith	*Karen Nicodemus*
Karolin Miranda	*Kayla Jones*
Keeghan Shropshire	*Kelsie Dean*
Kesha Patel	*Kilee Knight*
Nabeeha Khan	*Parth Vashi*
Q'May Qourters	*Reagan Musselman*
Robert Pokora	*Samantha Fritsch*
Sammy Omar	*Shannon Rychener*
Tashure Lott	*Timothy Pitts*
Tyra Latimer	*Zainab Nathani*

thank you
for finding my voice
for giving me room to breath
for giving me a home
for crying tears with me
for seeing me as more than the funny gay guy
but as the guy who has fought through hell
to get here today
thank you seeing my purpose
for letting me chase my dreams
for not backing down in the hard days
in the long days
in the days full of hundreds of essays
thank you
for the nights we spent at the club
dancing our hearts out
for the conversations and love
but most of all
thank you for letting me in
thank you for me

Table of Contents

Learning To Speak

It was within that moment
I knew I could learn
I knew I could grow
Because there was more

The Rising

My greatest fear was the power of myself.

this journey is just the beginning
it's going to be long
it will take years to accomplish
hard
treacherous
but worth it
so let's embark

The Rising

i had to run from that building
that place they called their home
out the doors
with the bells ringing
i had to run from them
calling me evil
saying i was going to hell
i had to run away
to run to my home

The Rising

Today was hard:
I walked into the hospital,
And for a couple minutes I had peace and
quiet.
But then I walked into the emergency room
And the pain hit me.
The hurt of those all around–
The patient holding on to dear life;
The wife kissing her husband goodbye one
last time;
The father and mother switching places to sit
by their son
Who they almost lost earlier today;
The lady who reviewed her diagnosis
And their eyes are filled with tears,
Because she didn't want to hear those words
from the doctor.
The old woman came in without know who
she was,
And the other cried that she couldn't breathe.
Even on the holidays
The pain is real,
And loss still exists.
And today I felt that toll.
It took a lot from me,
As I came in already under the weight of
everything
And just to see so many broken hearts.
I hope and pray they find their peace,
And broken hearts are made whole if just for
today.

The Rising

Today I looked through all the cards,
I read all the messages you wrote
From when I was younger.
It took me down memory lane,
Along all the roads from my younger self.
When you said you loved me,
And you said you were so glad I was your son.
When you said I was a good brother,
And you were always so happy for me.
But now I look around me,
And I see a card
That's says I can't be me—
Because that's what you had to tell me
For my birthday this year.
You keep trying to convert me
To your perfect, hurtful ways;
But I've learned that it's okay to be different.
I've paved my own way.
I am still loved—
And accepted—
It may not be by you;
You may have left me in the dust,
Despite your words:
But I am strong,
And I will conquer this.
Yes I cried,
Reading all those words;
I cried once again,

The Rising

To think of graduation past,
And how you never said congrats.
I don't understand it all,
And I don't understand why you had to turn
away.
I don't know where it fully changed,
And I became too horrible.
I don't know when the "I love you"
messages,
Just started to wear off.
But I know where it all ended.
I had to leave,
Because I couldn't take another beating.
I couldn't take another yelling,
I couldn't be locked in my room again for all
your rules;
That I learned were despicable within the
real world.
When I took my own paper to my room,
To write my own things—
It wasn't encouraged;
No I was yelled at,
And hidden for three months.
Maybe then you still said you loved me,
But was it still true?
I don't know!
All I know is now I'm covered in scars,
All over my skin and my heart;
And covered in ink so I can be okay.

The Rising

what is this
just another poem
just another spoken word
found in grief
and found in tears
but these words are words that show growth
slowly coming out of the ashes
this is the fourth Mother's Day i haven't
seen you
but also so it's been so much longer than
that
since i remember one that was happy
i've learned to slowly move on
o try to ignore this day
but i find myself writing this
while i sit in the car
waiting to go into my shift at the hospital
where i will see those mourning
and those in pain
some will have their mothers with them
and some will not
and even though most people don't
understand the pain i hold today
maybe some of them can
and i can comfort them
i can share their tears
and plant them in the field of growth i've
found exists
because i know it's still hurting

and i'm still crippled by the thought of today
but i can rise eventually
i sat through church today
i knew i had to go
if only to face the pain
i saw the roses passed around
to all the mothers
and i thought of you sitting at home
but i smiled for the others
And i only ran after the service
ran to my car
ran away
like i had done that day
i know i will keep trying to run away
but i hope one day i'll run to my own home
and feel safe

Another bottle of jack,
Maybe another sip of whiskey;
Another shot of whiskey on my desk.
All will be gone in the morning,
All will be drunken down.
Cuz I'm drowning myself in liquor
As I try to drown my feelings where I can't
see them.
Drank a six pack just tonight-
Couldn't feel a single thing,
Just depression.
The alcohol no longer works–
Doesn't take away my pain .
Cuz i been drinking every day,
Tryna ward my demons far away.
This drunken stupor in my eyes,
Makes me wanna hide away;
Wanna run to the car,
Smoke a cigarette
Drunk with this pain,
And drunk with the alcohol.
Maybe something will soothe it all,
Cuz this is what depression looks like for
me.

-alcohol-

The Rising

always
terrified
always
scared
if I walk out onto
the street
into the city
downtown
what will happen
will we all
become just another
fatality
will the gunman
choose my city next
while others look
on in complacency
everywhere you go now
we always have
to think
will
this be
the day
will this
be the place
it
all comes
too close to
home

(home)

The Rising

When will the fighting end?
When will I be able to stop crying?
When will the golden fields
Feel no more marching feet?
When will the bright blue sky
Not hear the blare of sirens?
When will the weeping mothers,
And screaming babas,
Not run and hide in tunnels?
When will the innocent blood of hundreds
Not coat the roads away?
It's only been two days-
But already I am exhausted.
I weep for my home country—
I weep for my people—
I see the city lights:
Blue and golden round the world.
Yet I still see the armies march,
And trample down the citizens.
My people are being destroyed,
The trident is weakening.
I am tired—
And I am worn—
And I have not fought.
But I have cried,
And watched my heart be torn
As my people become no more!

Sitting here alone in my car,
Just on a normal morning,
Waiting to go into work,
And the memory crosses my mind,
And suddenly I'm in tears again,
Crying my eyes out,
Gotta wipe them tho,
And walk into the world happy.
But suddenly I'm carried back to that moment,
Those hands on my body,
Unwelcome but still on my young skin,
The slur in her voice,
As she grabbed at me,
And didn't stop when the tears came down my cheeks,
That moment was eight years ago now,
But it will always be here next to me,
Haunting my every move,
Scared of a woman's hands,
Near my body,
The horror of that night,
That a woman,
Meant to love and cherish me,
Would violate me without a care in the world,
That moment cannot be forsaken,
Because I couldn't forsake you then,
At fifteen years old,

FIFTEEN

It's a tough world-
And I learned I'm going to fight it alone.
It's a tough one-
But my soul is against the rest.
Where you're casting me out for another,
Where you choose to make it easier for
others.
It's a tough world-
With the trauma in my heart.
Always feeling not safe to be myself.
It's a tough world-
Where I'm learning every day.
It's a tough world-
Holding on to everything;
Every moment that goes by,
I take it all away,
And learn day by day.
It tough world-
Trying to fend for myself.
It's a tough world-
But if I hide in the corner,
And make a dent in my wall:
Maybe one day,
It won't all seem so tough.

The Rising

eight years ago
a man walked into pulse nightclub with gun
seeking to shoot those who wanted a good
time
because he couldn't see past his closed
mind
he couldn't see how they deserved to live
so many had to die so soon
because he couldn't understand love
only hate was in his heart
that night
i wish i could turn back time
i wish we could have known what was going
to happen
i wish we could have warned my brothers
and my sisters
my family by life
that they were going to be attacked
eight years ago
a man walked into pulse
intent on hatred and debauchery
so many lost their heartbeat
while they danced on the floor
just trying to be themselves
¿why does hatred cast out authenticity؟
¿why does evil cast out love؟
the hatred in that mines eyes
left no room for truth and life
he couldn't understand another person's way

ho he sought to destroy them
a young man wept alone that night
as his love lay on the nightclubs floor
bleeding out
the first responders couldn't save them all
and a woman cried for her girlfriend's life
the queer
the different
my family
we deserve so much more
than to sit scared at home
not allowed to show ourselves
we want to walk down the street
holding the hand of another man or woman
we want to break the barriers of gender
without fearing a gun being held to our
temples
we want to be free
without being cursed in the street
we want to love
without being called a faggot
eight years ago that gun went off
eight years ago we lost so many of our family
but still today we walk around
scared of being seen
scared of hatred in another's heart
scared of evil in another's eyes

{pulse}

The Rising

dreams
catch the wind
fly away
turn around
float back
to me
then leave
again

The Rising

the beauty in the sad
love in the broken
and hope in the lost
heartbreak
destruction
demise
growth
hope
rebirth

be the change you
want to see
it's only one more year
you got
this
you have so
much ahead of you
going to be amazing
you have to
go through the hard
times to get to the good times

[got this]

The Rising

it's all fun

the laughing
the smoking
beer pong here
table tennis there
let's dance
–but house parties
are just curtains
on the windows of pain–

The Rising

this is your reminder
that my people are still dying
mothers holding children
babies screaming and crying for their dads
my friends and family are still hurting
having to run away from home
my people are still out their fighting
and my brothers are still sacrificing
i talk to my friends
and hear of all the horrors
i've seen the videos of my city
being swept to the ground
and i've seen the places i once walked
trod now by foreign foe

so when you ask me how my family is
and i say that they are fine
know that i say it out of exhaustion
for having to weep for my own country
and when you ask me how they are
please turn around and ask yourself
what are you doing for this frightful land
dying all alone

the people

out on the back porch
with a joint in my hand
laughing away
and i
thought these people were forever
i thought they were my besties
would walk through life forever
but they weren't
and that's okay

]forever[

The Rising

you ask me why I had to leave the church
because for years I lived in terror
in a place that preached love.
because for ages
i was told it wasn't abuse
because at least they weren't electrocuting
me.
i was told it was okay
because it wasn't a basement I was locked
in
it was just my bedroom.
at least I had food to eat
a sandwich a day
while they feasted on steak.
why did I leave
because your hands touching my body
was simply discipline
those beatings
all that yelling
and cursing
well it was to train me up in the right way
so one day i wouldn't depart from it.
but if one day i did
like julia over there
well it wasn't your fault
because you were the good parents.
why did I leave
because a book was preached from
and then used to hit me.

because when we had to stand naked in the
kitchen
it was the training of the lord.
so i had no other choice but to leave
so i wouldn't die.

{{religious}}

The Rising

I

W
A
K
E

From this

D
R
E
A
M

And I

R
U
N

For shelter

This dream

W
A
S

All too

R
E
A
L

it's just a drink a day
not enough to
get drunk.
not enough to lose it all
it's just one drink
every day
every damn day
every single night
every day
for a whole goddamn year.
or two
or three
well that's 365 days
times two
or three
or four
buts it's only one a day
so it must be okay

–suitable alcoholism–

maybe if I crush just one pill
just this once
just for this one occasion
i'll be fine in the future
cuz that's the way life works
habits
they are fake
all lies
i'll be fine
everything will be okay
just one pill
just one time
for all eternity
well maybe until next time
then just one pill then
and then again
and again
and wait
what happened
i'm a slave to it all
that can't be
it was just one time

–suitable drug use–

it's okay
you sank
deeper
deeper
down

till you
were gone
-forever-

<u>gone pt 1</u>

The Rising

i left
said goodbye
and now i'm free
i believe in a god
not yours
not your hateful
misogynistic
big man in the sky
i believe in the spirit
in us
around us
walking with the protestors
i believe
we can all find this deity
and not be chained
by a big man in the sky

[[religious healing]]

hell
what do I know
i don't know
but maybe
nothing at all

Conversations

I've learned
That hear in these lines
-It's just a simple conversation-
You and i
Changing the world dear
Join me
While we learn to converse
And set our voices free

this is the story of loss
of gain
and pain
when we were younger
i thought we were friends

The Rising

Sometimes I want to go out in the street,
And scream to the crowds what you've done
.
Sometimes I want to pick up the phone,
And call you;
Even though your in your church service,
Pretending to be good;
And I know you won't answer:
You won't hear my voice,
As I scream from the scars you've left in my heart.
I know you say you did what was right,
Cast me out of your sight.
You said it's okay,
To reject me for being me.
But what you didn't think about,
Was the pain that would leave.
You left scars in my heart,
Screaming each day.
It hurts when I walk home each night,
Without telling you my day:
And it's hurts when I'm feeling down,
And I know I can't call.
Maybe one day I will pick up the phone,
And pray that you answer;
And I'll tell you all the pain that you gave me,
And all the things you did wrong.
I know I'm not perfect,

And I made mistakes along the way;
I've tried to tell you my own,
And where I went wrong.
But all that matters is what you want,
And what you didn't get.
You flew thousands of miles-
To get a boy:
He was supposed to be perfect,
And live just like you.
You told him the money-
The cost that you bought him with-
Then reminded him daily that I wasn't
enough for that cost.
So maybe one day,
When I'm being strong:
And I'm firm in myself,
I'll learn to move on.
I'll pick the pieces,
That were left at your door.
I'll walk down the aisle,
And I know you won't be there
To smile at me.
And when I put on that cap,
At the end of my school;
I wish you'd be there,
To tell me you're proud.
But the truth is that doesn't matter to you,
Because I didn't turn out how you wanted,
So I just don't matter.

The Rising

I still hang that picture on the wall—
The picture of us all,
Standing by a fridge-
The fake forced smiles
Plastered on our faces.
It's the only thing I have of us.
I had to leave the rest behind.
When people ask for baby pictures,
I don't have those—
I don't have family vacations pictures,
Plastered through my phone.
Just one photo—
I hang on to.
And I know that if you knew I had that photo-
You would scream in horror.
Cuz those photos never left your care,
And you hated it all.
I wish you could see what that one photo
means,
And all the life held up together by one
picture.
Eighteen years in a five by seven!
But maybe it's okay,
Because who would want a picture of the
horrors,
Or a picture of the loss.
Maybe it's just me,
Clinging to every little thing,
Trying to feel like I matter.
It's just one picture,
But I still cling to it!

when i reach for the glass i've been
drowning all my feelings in
but it's empty
with only one drop left

every time i say
i'm a man
or call myself a man
i have to forgive myself
i am not a man
i am a person
i am free to be me
to call myself
what I am
and not bow
to how
the world
always
sees me

what i call myself

i've seen you looking at my page
watching my videos
and stalking my pictures
do you miss me
do you miss what we had
because i no longer miss it

i'm growing up
and i'm scared of it
i'm growing up
and i regret it
i'm growing up
and now i don't have time

i wish i could still sit at the piano
and play all the chords i wanted
i wish i could just go sit by the water
and relax for hours

but i'm growing up
and those days are gone

{{growing}}

The Rising

I've been trying to hide it,
And act like I'm okay.
I'll only cry alone at night,
Or in the morning with no one in the car.
I'll have a drink every night
Just to tell myself it will be okay.
But this pain of you going away,
Just for a year–
Is breaking me apart slowly.
I'm trying to hold it together,
And tell myself it'll be okay.
But sometimes that's hard to believe-
Sometimes it's hard to hold on to that.
When all I want to do is scream and cry,
So I'm laying here weeping;
Dreading the life it will be with you across the country.
But it will be okay;
So I'll cry at night,
And take a drink for you sir.

The Rising

This dichotomy in my head–
While I run from religion
(Run away from those organized groups,
Sitting in the church pews
And condemning me to hell)
While I still desperately seek for the open
doors
With bells ringing,
That will open their arms to me
Without knives behind their backs.
I seek to destroy the construct in my head,
And all around me–
I seek to forsake the church on every corner,
But I'm still seeking for the welcoming
sanctuary.
I am left to believe one thing–
I am seeking the truth of this religion they
speak of in the church.
I am looking for the authenticity–
Supposedly hidden somewhere in this belief
system.
I am seeking the love
They all speak of so well,
And yet still hide behind blackened lies of
hatred.
I am seeking to separate the religion,
From the christ.
I am seeking to destroy organized religion,
And seek the spiritual realm.
I want to believe
That this love exists somewhere;

The Rising

So I run past every corner,
And run from every sermon.
Still sitting in a pew once a month,
And then running away scared and
traumatized again.
Having to hide from the church again.
So this dichotomy continues on–
Running a new roundabout every Sunday,
Fighting down new steeples;
And erecting new open pews.
Maybe one day I'll wander out into the
meadow,
And find a people without this hatred in them.
One that takes me as spiritual-
And not religious.
And we won't have to break apart this
organization,
But until then I'll break down the rules in my
head.
These ideas forced on me from the
patriarchy–
From the misogynistic power hungry–
Until one day I'm free of religion,
And free in the spirit.

religious ruin

The Rising

I saw a seventeen year old today
Lying in the hospital.
He tried to take his life,
And my heart broke as he walked in.
I saw his mother sitting next to him,
These tears in her eyes-
The frantic look for help-
And honestly I was so happy to see her trying to get him help.
It made me glad to see her want to comfort him.
You could look into her eyes,
And see the shock at what had happened earlier in the day.
She had a flier in her hand–
Maybe this would help;
Maybe if she couldn't provide what was needed,
Someone else could.
In these young man's eyes,
I could see myself:
I could see myself at the darkest days,
With the tears and hopelessness in my eyes.
But in that mother I could see everything I longed for.
This Mother's Day she was fighting for her son,
More than anything she needed to keep him.

The Rising

Deployment isn't pretty,
It isn't fun.
Waiting for you
From so many miles away.
Waiting for that phone call,
Or that FaceTime when I can see you.
The nights of crying alone—
Trying to stay strong.
Going to work with a smile plastered on,
After weeping on the drive there.
But I know you're following your call,
And one day it will be worth it.
One day it will be okay—
That I can't go out with you:
That I can't dance at midnight with you.
One day these tears will pay off,
And the nights weeping alone on our couch,
And it will all be worth it.
One day the loss in my heart will be okay,
And we will be together.
But still this time isn't fun,
And I wish it didn't have to happen.

The Rising

The dichotomy of this moment–
Two men sitting on a bench:
One with privilege,
The other is just searching for survival.
He asked me for a cigarette–
But I don't smoke.
He asked for change–
But I don't carry cash.
I had failed this man!
I couldn't give him anything.
But he sat next to me–
And we ate our lunch in peace.
One man who has lost a lot,
But gained more:
And another who's lost a lot,
And searching for the way I found.
I hope I can guide him on the light,
When I can't give him anything!

The Rising

hold a gun to my head
pull the trigger
and it's over

The Rising

Why do we need pride?
Because when I fly my little flag,
Others curse at it.
Because when we go to the festival,
A old white man walks through trying to preach his gospel:
He thinks it's okay to yell at us all,
And condemn us to hell in the middle of the street.
Why do we need pride?
Because when I wear dress,
Old men say I am confused.
Why do we need pride?
To stand together as one family;
As old men in robes strip away the rights of humans.
Why do we need pride?
To help some of grow,
And help our younger queer selves heal.
We need to pride
To teach us pride;
And we need pride to let us live.
We will not be silenced!
We will not back down!
We are queer,
And we are proud!

The Rising

I saw your heart,
When you laughed me away at lunch;
Because you knew about the cuts on my arm.
Maybe that was the deepest of your bullying-
I know you had your own issues,
But laughing off mine didn't help me or you.
I saw your heart,
That afternoon after the funeral
Of one of the most important people in my life;
And you just questioned who I was,
And made excuses for my friend's actions.
I saw your heart,
When I tried to leave this life;
And you just yelled at me,
And told me how I made it a pain to you.
I saw your heart,
When you told me how it angered you to be on the phone dealing with me.
I saw your heart,
When you said you had hoped this had changed who I was.
I saw your heart,
When you didn't see mine.
I saw your heart,
When you didn't care about what happened to me;

The Rising

When you just asked for all the details,
And didn't care how it hurt me.
When you just yelled at me,
And destroyed everything.
I saw your heart,
But I'm glad I did-
Because I know to stay away,
Because you still have no regrets.

don't worry
it didn't work out in the end
just a broken story
and a broken heart
just another chance
for rebirth

The Rising

Walked in--
An old white man,
And I was scared.
Your hat called a liar to be our leader--
Called for hate to rule our land.
I know your type:
I've seen your people:
Breaking down barricades,
And telling me to die.
So I was scared--
The rainbow on my wrist,
Would it be too loud.
Would it yell out
"I am gay
Don't shoot."
Would you reply--
"Faggot
Go die alone."
So I was scared
Of the old white man.

how do i forgive myself
how do i grant grace
to my broken heart
how do i tell
myself
it's okay
how do i mourn
the moments i have lost
forever
how do i move on
how do i become okay
knowing it will happen
again
how do I say goodbye
to the memories i could
have made

all because
of my brain

i've learned i have to fight alone
i'll walk these streets with my head turned to the ground
i'll make a friend or two along the way
but i'll still drive on alone
as i take the turns in the road
staring into the night
i become content with this life
it's *okay* that i walk alone
it's *okay* that life has given me this path
trauma has taught me to fight alone
and not let anyone in
and even though some nights
i'll cry
at the end of the day
i'm proud of who i am
and keep walking through the days

–proud alone–

the boys in the hallway
damn they are hot
but my young mind
won't understand
that's okay
because it's not
i must hide
these thoughts
and just run away
so i wrote one of them a letter
stuck it in his locker
unsigned
did he know it was me
idk
did he hate me for it
idk
but i did it
then left the school
and never came back
cuz boys can't be hot

~~damn boys are hot~~

The Rising

Am I sad and depressed?
Why no–
Well not this moment,
But maybe the next one.
You see I'm breaking in these little shoes,
To run rampant across the mountains of life.
But these shoes were already tattered and torn
By years of mental sickness.
So no–
I'm not sad and depressed at one moment,
But maybe the next.
Some minutes I could scream from joy,
Seeing where I'm going–
The mountains I've crossed,
And ones I'm still bounding over.
But the next it may all crash down,
In a lonely disillusioned world.
Some days I hide it well,
Some days I just can't.
But that's okay,
Because I see where I've come from,
And what I've had to do.
But I also see where I am,
And the mountains that I have overcome.
I see the trenches that I wandered through–
The years of exile,
And I know that life will not all be easy from now on.
But I know what strength lies within me,
So though I may not be depressed right now,
It's okay if I am in a day!

The Rising

There's this battle in my head–
This conflict I must face,
Of where I should reside that's best for me;
But also best for everyone else.
Should I pave the way for others?
Should I tread this road,
With few others having gone before;
Just to wear it down more,
And break away more of the brambles
That those after me would see?
Or should I go to somewhere freely paved?
Where I can feel safe,
And where I can walk about without shame.
But I've come to this conclusion –
It's all a part of my healing.
No one path is correct–
No one road will heal it all–
The path I am on is meant for today,
It's meant so I can take this breath;
So I can live in this moment.
Not every way is easy–
It's hard to break down the brambles,
As more thorns grow up around me.
But I am here today,
And I will keep cutting down this sickness
around me.
But this road isn't where I'll always reside–
One day I'll walk away.
I will have done my part,

And move on to somewhere else–
Somewhere where the thorns have been fought,
Where only a few vines will entangle my feet,
And a place where I can finally be free.
It's okay that I'm exhausted of this fight,
It's okay that I'm tired of just fighting for the right to exist–
The right to be myself in this square mile.
It's okay that I'm worn out from this–
From every day having to fight to be okay,
To fight against those preaching against me,
Or every other person telling me sinning.
But I know in just a short time
I'll leave it all behind–
I'll walk out to greener pasture:
Not just ones that look greener,
But that I've tread upon before,
And I'll smile.
And heal my little heart some more.
But I am here now,
And I can breathe here now.

i was invited to go
celebrate your baby
come to the shower
but my anxiety came
and got the best of me
took away my joy again
took away my peace
left me hiding in the bathroom
shaking from fear
shaking because i couldn't
stand myself
so i left
before you even came
i still wished you well
over a text
still said congrats
through the phone
but i lost that moment
forever
one day
i'll pick up
all the pieces

the baby shower

let the bottle slip from your hand
let it crash on the floor
let it go
into a million pieces
we can clean up the shards
but we can't clean your heart
if you take one more sip
and go forever

–alcohol poisoning–

i feel like so many men
feel this fight
but run away
but today
i choose to stand
and fight myself
and those around

~male specimen~

touch me
feel me
caress me
or maybe not
if not that's okay
i understand
i'm not pretty
i don't have those pecs
i'm skinny
i'm a twink
and not everyone likes that
so it's ok
i'm pale
i'm bony
what's the word
ugly
that's what i am
so it's okay

–the twink–

The Rising

one day the party scene will crash
as you lay blackout drunk
and the next morning
you will never go back

The Rising

i needed to see myself
i needed to see others
so I could see myself
i needed to know it was okay
so i could go forward and do it
and many would say
i shouldn't wait to see another
i should just make a way
but i've lived my life making a way
so i could just survive
and there has come a day
where i can't make the way
some will follow in parts of my way
some will never have to even see it
but as i now walk down the road
already paved
i can still work
to make it wider
and smoother
but i needed to see another
to be myself
now i have hope

The Rising

Scared as a child--
Told I was a sin.
So now I carry around this guilt.
This shame of who I am;
The religion I was taught
Cast out all hope
For me to be me.
And yet you here--
Well-- you lived free
Without the religion of hate.
But rather one of freedom
And now you walk around
And don't carry the guilt,
The shame I feel.
You don't have to spend hours a day,
Rewriting that story in your heart.
You had love--
I had hate--
Both from the same place,
But in different ways.
I live scared,
And guilty.
You're free,
And loved.
So I'll run out the church,
While you run in.
One day it will be okay for both of us.

The Rising

i hope you know
one day i will close that door
block your number
And let you go
right now i still need you
and it hurts me
because this power
is just going to your head
but don't worry
it's fading away
and i am rising up
i will cry that day
when i say my last goodbye
but it's been coming
i've given you too much
let you pull me along
but it stops
the end

sometimes i still turn to the bottle
despite the voices in my head
telling me not to
telling me to go elsewhere
sometimes I still drink

The Rising

This morning I was able to wake up–
My heart was still beating,
And my lungs still breathe air.
I wasn't lying on the floor of a nightclub dead,
I wasn't being carried to the morgue–
From the classroom I'll never walk back into.
I wasn't just going to buy groceries,
And never come home.
It's still just the spring,
But the guns and violence have brought us through to winter.
Only five months of year are done,
But more than forty times that has a gun been shot into a group of people–
That's more than one a day;
And all those times,
More than one life has been lost.
One side says no guns:
The other says more guns,
Just different people.
But those bodies still lie in the morgue.
Thoughts and prayers are sent abroad,
But nothing ever changes–
The bodies still lie in the ground,
As the parents and families water the soil with their tears.
I drove by a school today,

And saw the children playing on the playground.
They were shouting with glee,
And running happily;
But I thought of the terror their parents faced,
When they let them out the front door this morning.
The tears they held back when their child got on the bus,
Praying to every god and deity they would be brought back safely.
Because some parents won't see their children run in the door again;
And some families won't hold their loved ones ever again.
This is the America we live in,
This is what happened to the American dream–
The land of freedom
Turned loose upon itself:
Where assault rifles are held by the young,
And carried straight to a little kid's head.
But where sanctity is held at disproportions,
And one can murder freely;
But another can't end the pain of rape.
This is the America we live in!
This is the America of the dying!
[spring 2022: RIP uvalde]

LMFAO
laugh my fucking ass off
or
LMAO
laugh my ass off
the amount of times i say this
text this
yell this across the hall
well i don't know
it's a lot
too many to count
my friends keep wondering how
i still have an ass
since i keep laughing it off
but i tell them it just keeps regrowing
it can't be that hard
just some muscles
and some fat
LMFAO
oops there i did it again
it's just so easy
a funny joke
and terrible story
i need to respond somehow
so why not
LMFAO
maybe add a few o's
so it just keeps coming off
LMFAO
maybe one day it won't regrow

The Rising

this month I wish I could hold you tight
i wish i could hold your hand at a parade
and go to parties out with you
but now you're hundreds of miles away
and this pride isn't the same
i wish i could show our love
everywhere i go to everyone
i wish i could kiss you in the middle of the street
or go to the pride party holding your hand
and dressed in a rainbow.
but i'm sitting here crying
cuz there's no one to go with to the pride party
cuz the gays all judge me for being alone
because i have this look on my face
of pure misery or anger
and i don't know which it is
is it anger at the world
for twisting fates this way
or misery at the gods
for turning our paths away
i don't know when i'll figure it out
but for now i know one thing
i can learn to be proud of myself
this month i'll have pride in myself
and hold your love still closer

{[¿happy pride?]}

The Rising

rapture terror
one day the lord is coming back
to take those he loves
and those he doesn't
well they are going to die of brimstone
and thus i stood paralyzed
every time the house was a little too quiet
i stood in terror
maybe the rapture happened
maybe i didn't quite make it
maybe i shouldn't have eaten yesterday
then i might be good enough to be carried
up to
the sky
so i lived scared of living

The Rising

To
find
yourself
you
must
sometimes
get
lost

they say i
can't hide
they say i can't always run away
but behind these words
i am
i can hide in
between the lines i write

~*thepoet*~

sometimes it's the little things
sometimes the bigger things
being alone at night
walking around the city alone
not going out to eat
cuz you can't sit with me
but no matter what it is
it's every day
not all day
some moments are okay
some moments I'm too busy to miss you
some moments life is too crazy
but don't worry
later that night i'll miss you
and wish i could be with you

deployed

The Rising

I was just ten years old
On my knees in church,
Saying that one day I would be a
missionary.
I would go out
And spread the word:
But I was told I couldn't like another boy,
And still go out into the world.
So I ran out of that church
As soon as I could--
Ran away from the church bells:
Away from the clergy
Standing pointing fingers
At the abomination I was:
And set free.
I ran from the pews
Lined with the Bible and hymnals,
Lined with the women in skirts
Telling me to be good--
To be a good husband,
Lead my family
In the way they sought.

missionary boy

The Rising

I've decided
I take every little journey in stride
Vegan
Slowly
Sober
Slowly
All of it
Slowly

The Rising

Today I saw the faces of the young girls
As they read the news captions–
Their rights stripped,
And their hearts bared to the public.
I saw the pain in their faces
As they saw old men decide their fates–
As they saw people in robes decide right
from wrong.
The whispers they shared,
Not knowing what side those around them
held;
Scared to start a debate,
Because the ground they stood on was
slowly slipping away.
I saw the uproar in the streets–
As a man
Said what to do with a girl:
As the decree came out:
So brutal,
So removed from the people,
And my heart breaks with the masses
Wondering what comes next?
Old men in robes,
Decreeing laws
To protect the guns,
And destroy the helpless.
What has this country come to?
What is the difference between the church
and state,

When they are molded into one?
What are Christians doing,
Forcing their faith on another?
What is this love?
It's not love–
I can tell you that!
It's a burning passion,
To destroy those that are different.
So my heart groans with the broken;
And I weep with the birthing of the world,
As their rights are stripped away.

the birthing

The Rising

I am scared and terrified.
Just last night I danced my heart away
In a young gay club,
As I saw the drag queens walk out on stage
And dance with us.
I felt healing in that moment for my young
queer heart;
It was a moment of salvation for the hurt
gay boy inside;
It was a moment I desperately needed–
To feel loved and accepted,
To feel wanted to those around me,
And to feel seen and heard just being
myself.
But then this morning my heart was broken,
As I saw rights stripped away from humans.
And I wondered what would come next?
They started taking these rights,
And then started questioning others.
Will I be able to stand openly with my
fiancé?
Will I be able to marry the love of my life?
With Obergfell fall,
And with it my right to marriage?
I am terrified of what will happen,
Scared that I will see my hopes and dreams
destroyed–
All the work of those before fall down.

The deaths of all those before will not be in vain tho,
The queer elders will not have passed on for nothing-
I will walk through the street.
We will all walk together!
There will be a larger riot than ever before!
Because my forefathers did not fight for nothing–
They fought for me!
And I will fight for those after me!
To pave this road in a rainbow;
And if my blood lie along that road,
So be it–
I will not let this go without a fight!

~the rainbow battle~

The Rising

i can't wait till i'm all grown up
until i've found my community
my career and a place to settle down
i want to be with friends and feel happy
but I know when i am there
i will regret these days
not taking hold
and carrying with each one
a memory dear
<u>*so i will embrace today*</u>
<u>*while i stride towards tomorrow*</u>

I haven't found this end road of sobriety
Haven't found my peace with it all
Haven't found a calm outside

i feel like you deserve to know the pain i feel
you know that i still cry
And that though I've rebuilt my life
there's still cracks in my walls
and some of the shingles fall off the roof
but it's okay
cuz apparently i'm the *bad guy*

`hell`

The Rising

if you're not white
male
cis
het
then sit down

that's what i heard
from the balcony
and that's when i left
with the throng
not listening to another word

the balcony voices

The Rising

it's kinda funny
how i'll hide behind these words
and you will never see me
but you will know my heart
soul
and life

**my all**

it's weird to me
not in a bad way
its just weird
it's been over a year

The Rising

you asked me what tied me to this city
and i said my fiancé
to which you asked what "*she*" did
i simply replied with a "*they*"
and you once again said "*she*"
i said "*they*" yet a third time
and finally you said
oh does your fiancé go by "*they/them*"
to which i said
somewhat quietly and scared
"it's a *him*"
and you said 'oh that's okay
i know pronouns are important
And i'm learning more and more myself"
but now i'm looking back
and i see a greater fault
in this world
others will assume the world is straight
assume that we are all
what they consider normal
and will this close off the space for
differences
the different must fight for room
to share these differences
the world should open up the way
without gender
without the guidelines
open up that space
for anyone to be themselves and safe

refer to my fiancé as "*they*"
until i feel safe to say "*him*"

"they/them"

it's hard some days
crying in the car
on the way to work
but i have wipe it away
and go into work

—work—

You lost your faith in first loves--
Lost your faith in the first boyfriend,
In the first love:
And now only utter warnings.
Scared of broken hearts,
Scared of things falling apart.
Where did this flame go?
Where did the fire feeding a first love
Fly away to?--
That now you say it isn't good,
That now you don't trust
And say to wait.
Why do you turn around,
And believe in the heartbreaker?
And not the healer?
Why does first love
Equal failure:
Connected with not fighting to the end.
This is a first love--
But it will last.
So have faith--
I know you've seen the stories
And news of how they failed--
How they fell apart--
How the end of it came swiftly.
But for every horror
Twenty more dreams become reality.
So have faith
In the first love!

FIRST LOVE

The Rising

circular
winding
ups
and downs
and another up
but never a line

//circular//

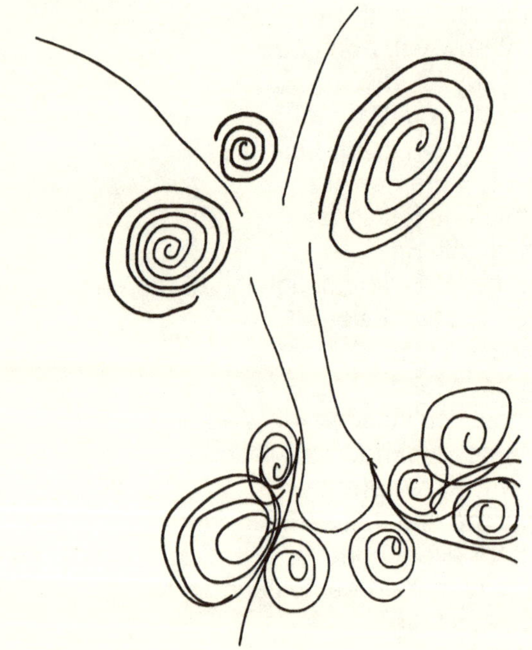

The Rising

sobriety
california sober
alcoholic
i don't know which is best
i like to think i'm okay being *california sober*
nothing too hard
nothing that takes away from my life
all my priorities
but i still feel guilt
maybe i'm just an *alcoholic*
i don't waste my days away drinking
but i don't stop having a drink once a day
i don't know
i probably never will

this is a high
this is growth
but this won't be forever
and that's okay
another rush will come
crashing me down
but i hope to remember
this high

/~high~/

The unique experience
Of the gay--
The first boyfriend
So many think you have;
Isn't really your first.
You had one or two more
Hidden in the closet--
Unable to let anyone know.
But they were there,
And you grew from their failures
And the hopes.
So when another see you here,
And thinks it's your first.
You know you have experience,
And your not fully blind.

<u>hidden boyfriend</u>

but a new person
arose
and took over
the real you
was able
to be resurrected
when you said goodbye
forever

gone pt 2

Deliberate Voices

I've learned I have a voice
I've learned how to talk
I've learned I have power
Just in these words
And now I will shout
From the rooftops
To the gutters
My voice and power
Can change the day

some tell me to be quiet
and that i don't need to bring it all to light
i need to think of all the shame i'll bring to people
or all the bridges i will burn
but i've thought of all that
and they are better burnt today

maybe one day we can rebuild
but it's rotting now
and the more people who walk across
the more people destroyed
so i will yell
and i will shout
this is not the end

burn the bridge!

The Rising

i see my growth
i've seen my change
i've fought battles
and won
and i know
i've had an easier time healing than many
i've made it here faster than others
i've been privileged
and i am thankful
so please remember on your darkest days
it's just another down
there will be an up
and another one
it takes time to heal
takes time to mend

your voice
you never
know how
far it will go
never know
how loud
it can sound
until you use it
until you learn
one day
you have it
until one day
you step out
and say this
i have a voice
i have found my voice
you never know
until you use
it

<u>The voices</u>

The Rising

Some nights are like this one tonight–
Thankfully it doesn't happen as often now.
But I've learned to embrace it when it
comes:
Embrace the tears,
Embrace the loneliness,
Embrace the pain deep inside;
And find myself.
I dive deep within,
And look around my heart.
Sometimes I have to walk through the
rooms of my past;
I have to peek through the closed windows
in my heart,
And look into the dark shadows of years
gone by.
It's okay for me to be here,
It's okay to look at the past,
And look to the future shaking in my boots.
So I will lay here,
Sleepless and alone;
And I will learn to rejoice in this moment.

The Rising

I'm learning to be proud of who I am,
By pouring myself into working for all.
I'm learning to heal the scars in my heart,
By giving a voice to all those who don't.
I will stand up at rallies!
I will shout from rooftops!
Maybe my own little voice-
Screaming loud through the fields,
Will heal this poor heart
Torn by so many voices and haters.
I'm learning to change,
To come out from hiding-
To let everyone know not to fuck with my
heart.
Cuz if you mess with mine,
You mess with a whole community.
And I will not bow down to your hatred,
I will not bow down to your misogyny.
I'll slowly overcome this fear of myself;
I'll overcome this desire I have to hide;
I'll overcome the pain deep in myself,
Sown from years of despise.
I am the change!
I am a voice!
And we will go on together,
To heal all the young hurting hearts I can,
And put my broken spirit together again.

The Rising

I sat in the car today
And thought of my life–
Of all the dreams I had,
And all the hopes I held dear.
How one day just four years ago,
I sat for hours locked in a room crying,
And picking apart the chimney.
But today I walked into a hospital
And worked with the doctors team.
How I am working to help bring healing and hope,
Something my younger self desperately craved.
This is my life!
This is my dream!
This is what I desperately craved!

here's your reminder
to forgive yourself
for your mental health
to forgive yourself
for the times you couldn't go
for the times you bailed last second
for the anxiety attacks
in the bathroom five minutes before
it's not your fault dear
that your brains fucks with you
that way
mourn those moments lost
mourn when you can't go
and do something
you know
you would have always cherished
but then forgive yourself
hold your heart
hold the crying and screaming
for that moment
and hold your brain
wrenching from fear
it's not your fault
it's not your fault

~with love~

anxiety filled person

The Rising

Today is June 1st–
The rainbows will all be taken out,
And pride will be popular again.
But is this truly pride?
Or just a business scheme?
Because queer people still exist
Every day of every year.
So please think before you act.
We are still here in July,
December,
And April;
Just as much as today!

i had to let that little boy go
had to let him run
unlock the door
and say goodbye
so maybe one day
i could see him come back
all grown up
and happy in his skin
i had walk away
let the past be the past
and never look back
i had to let the tears fall
and wave as he left
i knew
i would never see him again
if he didn't leave that day
to find himself

]]growing up[[

i came out two years ago
said i was gay and proud
but it's been a hard two years
because i've learned so much about myself
i've opened up my deepest secrets just to
myself
and seen how much more i am

<u>gayandproud</u>

The Rising

some moments I'm okay
and others i just break down
this morning i cried my time away
thinking of what the future holds
and feeling that ashen taste on my lips
but now I taste the honey on my lips
and the tears are gone
just a few hours ago i couldn't hold myself
together
but now i'm fine
and smiling to everyone
so i guess i'll be okay
cuz i can handle it all in hours
and go day by day

~~BPD~~

just because
you see such growth
in yourself
don't hate them
when they don't
grow at the same rate

leaving isn't bad
saying goodbye
and closing a door
isn't wrong
it's healing
it's love
so close that door
and don't look back
it's you
not them

the right goodbye

The Rising

Writing scripted lines that mock you–
Those that poke fun at you,
And lack the respect you think you deserve.
That's what you claim of me:
Your verdict of why I don't deserve you
Are the words that I write to the world.
Uncovering your lies.
You hid me in your family for years,
And strutted me around at the store
As your perfect servant:
But behind closed doors it all fell apart,
And now you're scared
Cuz you feel called out
And don't know what to do.
So you call me a liar,
And tell me I'm mocking you;
Because your facade is falling down,
And your tapestries that cover the windows
of your life
Are all being ripped down,
So now others will see inside,
And will know the wars inside your home.
They will see the dictator you brought to
judge.
I'm not here to mock you–
I'm here to heal,
And end the pain.
So maybe another young boy feels heard,
And feels understood:

The Rising

Another young child
Will find the healing
After mom flogs them,
And dad yells all the curses possible.
I'm not here to mock you,
But to call you out
In a way that you will never understand.
Maybe you will be called to Justice one day
For all the nights I starved locked away,
And the insanity that trails along every
single word you say to me.

sometimes you have to be content
content with what you've done
because even though
you want to have the loudest voice
and make the greatest change
if you've done all within your range
and wielded all the power that you can
then you have reached the gates of
contentment

The Rising

Growing up–
I was always taught
That those people were weird:
The men who liked other men,
The women and loved another woman,
Those who couldn't choose their gender–
They were the weird people,
They were different–
The perverted,
The outcasts;
They didn't belong,
And they needed to be fought against.
The government needed to hate them,
And obliterate them.
And slowly I realized I was one of them–
Year after year I saw that maybe I was one of them:
Maybe I was the weird one;
And when I came out,
I thought I was still the weird one.
I was proud of myself,
But still the weird one.
I couldn't love a woman,
I didn't fit in my gender–
Therefore I was the outcast,
And this lead me to always be scared.
Terrified that I wasn't normal enough.
It was okay that I existed–
I just had to exist in this bubble:

The Rising

This bubble outside the world,
This bubble where the outcasts lived.
But time and date sought to show me otherwise.
We aren't weird,
We aren't perverted,
We aren't any more different than anyone else.
Maybe those who don't accept us–
Those who see us as the outsiders;
They are the weird ones.
We belong just as much as anyone else.
We belong in government.
We belong in the churches,
In the synagogues,
And in the mosques and temples.
We belong out in the streets,
Holding hands
Just like the straight couples.
We deserve to be on the front cover of a magazine,
Proudly kissing our love.
We aren't the weird ones–
They are the weird ones.
The ones who can't see us for us,
And who can't accept that we exist
And will continue to exist.
The ones who have decided we destroy society,

While we share love and patience to every individual.
They are the outcasts;
And with this simple fact came freedom.
Freedom to be me,
Freedom to be proud;
But more than proud–
To be okay,
To be myself and be alright,
To not shy away.
Yes I'm still scared–
Scared of the haters and abusers of righteousness.
Yes I walk around looking left and right,
Looking to see who is laughing,
Or yelling out insults at my gender identity.
And no maybe I won't be on the front page of a magazine–
But we don't all need to be.
We just need to be walking the streets,
And learning to live–
To breathe–
To trod the same dust as everyone else,
And not be scared of who will hate to see our footprints.
Growing up I was taught wrong,
But as I heal I learn the right.

The Rising

Stop stalking me
Trying to find out what is going on in my life
You hire them to look at what I post
And send it all to you
You use the internet to find info
And try to store it away
But what is it doing
For you or for me
Half of what you find is twisted somehow
Turned in an amalgam of truth and falsity
And your prying eyes don't stop me
And don't help you
So please find something better to do with your time
Find something better to look into
You can ask me the questions you want
But for the love of all that is good
Just stop stalking
And stop looking around web corners for more information
It will only make you more resentful
That I am living free
And growing each and every day
And you will just watch your power scheme fall away
I hope you see this
I hope you read it
And it hits your core
And chases you far away
Never to return to my page
Whether it's you
Or your spies

"He/They"
but you hear
"He/Him"
okay that's easy you say
i can use *"him"*
cuz that's just *"normal"*
you think *"they"* isn't important
if i say both
that means only one to you
but i said
"He/They"
i never said i preferred one over the other
i'm asking just one simple thing
step out of your comfort zone
so i can step into mine for a single second
Thank you.

with love,
He/They

slowly
surely
i am
working to be
better
working to be
prouder
and happier
goodbye
to the old person
to the old me

losing my religion
one piece of my heart at a time
forsaking all that past
breaking my heart
to heal my soul
i've lost my religion

but you'll piss them off
the politics
the religion
you might make them angry
but i don't care
it's not my job to make them happy
it's not my job to always make them feel
good
so i'll piss them off
the political parties can yell at me
they are upset
because i found my voice
and i use it

The Rising

Recovery
Rebound
Release

The Rising

You are still worthy
Despite years of in grown hate
Despite years of outward defeat
Despite hours upon hours
Crying in the car
Alone
You are worthy
You are still worthy
Despite the man who told you
You weren't good enough
Despite the mother who told you would
never be
Enough
Despite the father
Who beat your back
For failing in one small thing
Despite the boyfriend
Who told you he didn't love you anymore
You are still
Worthy
You are worthy
Despite the world
Telling you
You don't belong
You are worthy
Despite the men
All around
Telling you to be quiet
To sit down
To be obedient
You are worthy
You are still worthy
Despite

The Rising

i'm twenty one
seen a lifetime though
lived through centuries
at twenty-one
my heart is cold as stone
fortified like the mayan ruins
all because of what i've seen
and what i've lived

young and old

The Rising

I'm learning to love this skin–
This body-
This spirit.
This person that I am:
To love my emotions,
All the wide ranging sea of them.
The smile and laugh that is louder than a
foghorn.
I'm learning it's okay,
That my emotions take large sways;
And it is all going to be okay.
As I run along through life–
On down the years ahead of me,
I am slowly learning to embrace myself.
The fact that when I laugh:
It's loud–
It's boisterous–
It might be awkward,
But it will make you smile.
When I feel an emotion:
It's as strong as a river–
And will overcome all else;
But this is my strength–
The power to love so strongly,
The ability to hate so strongly
That it will propel me forward to action.
It's okay that others don't understand what's
inside my head,

Or what happens when I think a simple
thought.
It's going to be alright–
If everyone doesn't feel the same passion,
And won't comprehend the way my
chemicals work.
I am learning to be happy in my skin,
And in my mind.
To be myself–
Full of emotions–
Loud when laughing–
And unable to be tamed!

The Rising

I think I'm addicted:
Addicted to the thrill–
The stress–
The next movement–
The
Next wave.
One ends,
And I crash fully until the next.
I don't know what a break is:
I don't know what time off is.
I've never known what summer is,
So it doesn't exist for me.
I never got a fall break,
Or a spring break,
Or a winter break;
So that just doesn't exist in undergrad.
It's project after project,
I guess this prepares me well
For future life–
For the project I will undertake–
For mountains I will climb.
I'm addicted to the climb:
To the going:
To the running.
Even when I'm tired,
I'm still going.

The Rising

I've tried to throw the bottle out,
And trash the vape down the storm drain;
That way I have to quit.
Sometimes I even can
(For a few days,
Or a couple months)
But then I'll find myself
Back inside that store,
Buying a new device,
Some new juice for the pods.
I'll go buy the liquor place–
Another keg of whiskey,
A bottle of vodka.
I quit for a while,
But I don't know if I can do it forever.

teenage dream
the fantasy
that i am walking through
healing
growing
chasing
after everything
i cry
for my sixteen year old
heart
that never thought
i could do this
that boy
who sat in a corner
with a blade in his hand
and drew art on his arm
but i'm thankful
for him
cuz without it
i wouldn't be here today

The Rising

carpe diem
seize the day
you have the power
you have the strength
take control
carpe diem

life will never stay the same
embrace the change
flow
grow
change

The Rising

i've heard maybe it's a dream
maybe it's just a joke
moving past that talking stage
moving past the physical
the one night stands over and over again
just sleeping with the same guy
multiple times
but only seeing his body as good
but maybe its more than a dream
maybe it can be reality
with you

The Rising

I had to turn away;
I had to leave for work.
Hug you one last time before you left.
I was trying to hold it all together,
As I walked out that door–
As I walked off that base,
Past the other families
Not yet leaving.
I had to have a brave face,
Only one tear or two.
But as soon as I walked out those doors–
It all flowed.
I couldn't hold it together any longer.
I wept that whole drive home.
I know it's only a year,
But it's been the longest year of my life.
That sweet goodbye,
I love you,
And I will stand here for this year;
Next to you.
Please come back home.

holding me tight
your hands on my thighs
touch me slowly
down my chest
and over my waist
just one more scream
just call me babe one more time

The Rising

my favorite spot in this apartment
the pictures of us hanging
right below the flags
the rainbow and the trident
side by side in the basket
the record player
and the pictures
it is my home
it is me in just one corner
y music
my words
you and i
and that old hateful family just poking out
buts it's all me
and i love it

The Rising

It's the slow calm voice
It's the haunting breaths in my ear
It's the smell of ice coffee in the morning
It's the times you run to the store
While I get to keep sleeping
It's the times we fight
And you don't leave me
It's the words you say
When we both have to battle
My mental illnesses
It's the hours
We discuss what to do for the day
Until there's two hours left of sunlight
Its every day
Every year
For lifetime
And i'm in love with it
I'm in love with you

The Rising

i felt you next to me
traced my fingers along your chest
and laid my head to rest on your chest
while I stared into your eyes
and knew I was going home

sometimes i just sit back
and i get to think
about how one day
i'll wear a ring tied to you forever
how one day
i'll call you husband
be able to stand up in a crowd
and proudly call you mine
my spouse
my forever
my home
my love
one day i won't have to wake up
and not be able to call you all mine
one day will be forever
and i'm so thankful
you are my husband

The Rising

that night
up on the mountain
you held me next to you
as i rested my head on your shoulder
and we kissed
looking down at the city lights
that night as we laid under blankets
and our naked skin touched
that spark between us
between our lips
that couldn't be kept apart
as i saw your muscles ripple through your chest
that was the beginning of coming home
that was the start of a home

let's go dancing in the club
feel your body next to mine
as the music pulses through our veins
i want to hear your breath in my ear
soft but harsh
luscious and sweet
i want to see the sweat drip down your
chest
bared by unbuttoned shirt
let's go to club
will you dance with me

The Rising

i needed to see we exist
we are out in the streets
not just hiding in the apartments
but out at the restaurant
dancing at the club
with each other
and i saw this
so i am okay
because I know
we are no longer the lost
the hidden
we are loud
and so am i
nothing to be ashamed of

we are everywhere

so please don't ever
let the old you back
don't take those chains
back
don't walk
back
you deserve today
not them
Forever

gone pt 3

The Rising

goodbye
until next time
until i bear my heart again
until you hear from me again
goodbye
it's been lovely
letting you in
behind my closed doors
through the windows of my verse
goodbye
you will be okay

About the Author

Sergiy Abelson (they/he) was born in Ukraine and adopted to the United States. From a young age he showed a love for words and writing and began writing. During high school, he began writing poetry daily and quickly stockpiled hundreds of original poems. Having written well over a thousand poems, he has began compiling them into collections to share with the world. He feels that he can communicate easier in poetry than in prose and loves sharing his work with the world. He hopes that his small voice will help others heal and pave the way throughout the world. Much of his poetry

surrounds LGBTQPIA+ rights, healing from trauma, and living life free of the past.
The original artwork included throughout the book is meant to reflect the nature of poetry. Sergiy enjoys writing poetry in such a way that leaves much of the interpretation up to the reader, and this applies also to the artwork. Meant to capture the moment in chilling secrecy, yet let the reader interpret in their own views. He uses a sketching simplistic style that allows the viewer to see the grandeur of life and themselves through the art.

www.ingramcontent.com/pod-product-compliance
Lightning Source LLC
LaVergne TN
LVHW041103150826
845673LV00007B/1905

* 9 7 9 8 8 4 6 1 0 0 4 0 4 *